W9-AVR-635

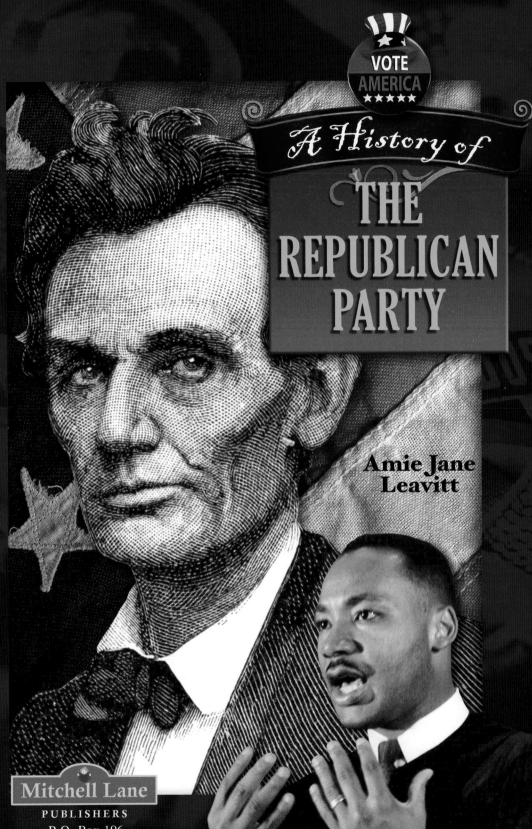

VOTE
AMERICA
★★★★★

A History of

THE REPUBLICAN PARTY

Amie Jane
Leavitt

PUBLISHERS
P.O. Box 196
Hockessin, Delaware 19707

A History of the Democratic Party
A History of the Republican Party
A History of Voting Rights
A Kid's Guide to the Voting Process

Copyright © 2013 by Mitchell Lane Publishers

Printing 1 2 3 4 5 6 7 8 9

Library of Congress Cataloging-in-Publication Data

Leavitt, Amie Jane.
  A history of the Republican Party / by Amie Jane Leavitt.
     p. cm. — (Vote America)
  Includes bibliographical references and index.
  ISBN 978-1-61228-261-9 (library bound)
  1. Republican Party (U.S. : 1854-)—History—Juvenile literature. I. Title.
  JK2356.L43 2012
  324.273409—dc23
                                          2012007536

eBook ISBN: 9781612283388

PLB

CONTENTS

Chapter 1

"A House Divided ... Cannot Stand"

On a warm autumn day, two men walked into the Illinois Statehouse in Springfield. One was thin and tall, about 6 feet 3 inches. He was wearing a short-sleeve shirt and loose-fitting trousers. His face was weathered from the years he had spent working in the sun. The other man was just the opposite. He was nearly a foot shorter at only 5 feet 4 inches tall. He was chubby and round. The smooth, rosy skin on his face proved that he had spent very little time working outdoors. His tailored clothing was neat and trim.

The tall man was a practically unknown Illinois lawyer named Abraham Lincoln. The other was Stephen A. Douglas, a famous Illinois senator. They were opposite not only in appearance, but in ideas too.

On this day, October 4, 1854, Lincoln stood on a platform and spoke. He talked about the Kansas-Nebraska Act that Douglas had encouraged Congress to pass in May 1854. The Kansas-Nebraska Act would let people decide whether to allow slavery in the northern territories. Many people were very upset by this new act, and Lincoln was one of them. He did not think that slavery should move into new parts of the

Statues of Abraham Lincoln (left) and Stephen A. Douglas in Washington Park, Ottawa, Illinois, near the site of the first of the 1858 Lincoln-Douglas debates.

A political map of the United States in 1850 shows free states (red), slave states (brown), and the vast territory in which the right to own slaves was yet to be decided.

country. In fact, during this speech, Lincoln made a very important announcement. He proclaimed for the first time in public that he didn't think slavery was right at all, anywhere. Douglas believed that people should have the right to own slaves and take them wherever they wanted, like any other kind of property. Lincoln believed that a country could not be half slave and half free. Lincoln's words left a powerful impression on many of the people who were in the audience that day.

Just a few months before this event, on March 1, 1854, a group of people met in an old schoolhouse in Ripon, Wisconsin. They, too, felt like Lincoln. They didn't agree with the Kansas-Nebraska Act. They talked about slavery and about keeping the northern territories free for settlers. By the time they left that night, they had all agreed to form a new political party. They felt that none of the current political parties represented their views. They named their new party the Republican Party.

The Republican Party was founded in the Little White Schoolhouse in Ripon, Wisconsin. The schoolhouse has been a National Historic Site since 1974.

Many people in the Northern states felt the same way as these new Republicans in Wisconsin. They became Republicans, too. Branches of the Republican Party popped up all across the North.

Lincoln wasn't yet a member of the Republican Party when he gave his speech on that warm October day in 1854. But he would become one of its most important leaders. In fact, six years later,

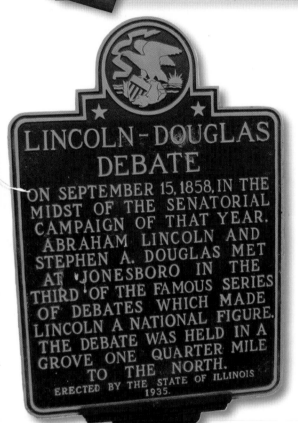

LINCOLN-DOUGLAS DEBATE

ON SEPTEMBER 15, 1858, IN THE MIDST OF THE SENATORIAL CAMPAIGN OF THAT YEAR, ABRAHAM LINCOLN AND STEPHEN A. DOUGLAS MET AT JONESBORO IN THE THIRD OF THE FAMOUS SERIES OF DEBATES WHICH MADE LINCOLN A NATIONAL FIGURE. THE DEBATE WAS HELD IN A GROVE ONE QUARTER MILE TO THE NORTH.

ERECTED BY THE STATE OF ILLINOIS 1935.

in November 1860, he was the first Republican to be elected president of the United States. This election was important not only for the Republican Party, but also for the history of the nation.

Lincoln once said, "A house divided against itself cannot stand." He was right. The United States was divided on the issue of slavery. Republicans, for the most part, were antislavery. They had supporters in many parts of the country, but not in the South. When Lincoln was elected as the 16th president, the South wasn't happy. One by one, the Southern states announced that they were seceding, or leaving the union. By the time Lincoln took office on March 4, 1861, the Southern states had already formed their

Platform of the Early Republican Party

Do not allow slavery in the northern territories
Give free homesteads in the West to farmers
Improve public education
Place taxes on goods coming from other countries
Help new immigrants become citizens
Build a railroad to the Pacific

own country. They called it the Confederate States of America. They had chosen a Democrat—Jefferson Davis—as their president. Civil War was declared.

Early Republican Heroes

The Civil War lasted for four years. During that time, Lincoln left his mark as one of the most influential presidents the country has ever known. He appointed people to his cabinet who were the best qualified for the job. It didn't matter that many of them had once been his political rivals. To understand what was happening in the war, he went to the front lines to visit his generals and the troops. He wrote letters to the families of fallen soldiers. He gave powerful and memorable speeches that he re-searched and wrote himself. In 1863, he freed the slaves with the Emanci-pation Proclamation. Many Northerners said his leadership saved the Union.

Lincoln was one of many impor-tant Republicans during the Civil War Era, as well as Frederick Douglass, who was born a slave and escaped to freedom when he was eighteen. In the North, he joined a group

Frederick Douglass

First Reading of the Emancipation Proclamation of President Lincoln by Francis Bicknell Carpenter. A proclamation is an executive order issued by a U.S. President.

of abolitionists, or people against slavery. Douglass was a writer, editor, and speaker. He was a friend and adviser to President Lincoln. After the war, he worked with five more Republican presidents in many important positions.

Clara Barton spent her life serving others. When the Civil War broke out, she nursed wounded soldiers—even those on the front lines. After the war, Barton helped thousands of missing soldiers find their way home. She founded the American chapter of the Red Cross. She helped campaign for many Republican presidential candidates, including James Garfield.

Clara Barton's Red Cross Photo

Improving the Country

Slavery wasn't the only issue important to the early Republicans. They also wanted to help improve settlements and transportation in the West. They wanted to encourage immigration and help business owners with special tax rates. They also wanted more people to get an education. The Republicans accomplished many of their early goals while the nation was at war.

In 1862, the Republican Congress passed the Homestead Act. This gave 160 acres of free land in the West to people who were willing to farm them. Many people in the East filled their wagons and rushed westward to claim their free land.

Lincoln signed the Homestead Act of 1862. Anyone who had never taken up arms against the U.S. government, including freed slaves, could apply for a federal land grant. In order to keep the land, homesteaders had to improve the land, live on it for at least five years, and then file for the deed of title.

VOTE

Republicans feel that it is important to take care of military veterans and their families. This policy has been part of the party's platform since 1864.

That same year, the Morrill Act was passed. Also called the Land-Grant College Act, it granted land for building colleges and universities. Massachusetts Institute of Technology, Cornell University, and the University of Arizona are just a few of the dozens of colleges that benefited from this program.

Republicans wanted to build a railroad to connect the East to the West. This Transcontinental Railroad would make it easier to cross the wild frontier. They passed the Pacific Railroad Acts of 1862 and 1864. In 1863, workers began laying tracks. One company, the Central Pacific, worked east from California. Another company, the Union Pacific, worked west from Missouri. The two raced to see who could lay the most track. They met with great fanfare on May 10, 1869, in Promontory, Utah.

Rebuilding the South

On April 9, 1865, Southern General Robert E. Lee surrendered at Appomattox Court House, Virginia. The Civil War was finally over. Hundreds of thousands of Americans had been killed. Towns, railroads, and farms were destroyed.

The period after the war was called Reconstruction. The Republicans were split on the best way to handle the South during Reconstruction. One group of Republicans, which included President Lincoln, wanted to rebuild the South, free the slaves, and move on. The other group, called the Radical Republicans, believed that the South should be dealt with firmly. Southerners had caused the Civil War, so they should be punished for it. The Radical Republicans also believed that freed slaves should become citizens, and the men should be able to vote.

There was a grand celebration at Promontory, Utah, when the tracks laid by the Central Pacific and Union Pacific Railroad companies were joined with a golden spike. With the country connected from coast to coast, people could travel across the United States in days instead of months.

Lincoln did not have a chance to promote his group's ideas. On April 14, 1865, just five days after Lee surrendered, Lincoln was shot by Southerner John Wilkes Booth. He died the next day. No one knows for sure, but things might have worked out very differently for the South had Lincoln not been assassinated.

During Reconstruction, the Radical Republicans passed laws that made life very difficult for former Confederates. The South was divided into districts that were governed by the military. The Southern states had to write new constitutions. They had to show they were loyal to the country before they could be readmitted to the Union. Former Confederate supporters could not hold office. The Radical Republicans also passed laws that helped the freed slaves, including the Thirteenth, Fourteenth, and Fifteenth Amendments to the Constitution.

A More Perfect Union

On the bright spring morning of March 31, 1870, Thomas Mundy Peterson rose at daybreak and started his daily chores. He worked in the barn, cleaning the stalls and feeding the horses. After a while, his employer, J. L. Kearny, came to talk to him.

"You really should go exercise your citizen's privilege," he told Peterson.

Thomas had almost forgotten. Just the day before, the Fifteenth Amendment to the U.S. Constitution had gone into effect. Now, African-American men could vote. The people in his small town of Perth Amboy, New Jersey, were voting today on an important issue for the town. Now Peterson would be allowed to vote with them!

After eating his lunch, Peterson walked into town. He entered the small building where the voting was taking place. He was handed a ballot. Peterson looked at his two options, marked his decision, and placed his ballot into the box. That was it. He had officially voted.

This may seem like a simple action, but it was actually significant. Peterson had just become the first African American to vote in the United States.

HARPER'S WEEKLY.

A JOURNAL OF CIVILIZATION.

VOL. XI.—No. 568.]   NEW YORK, SATURDAY, NOVEMBER 16, 1867.   [SINGLE COPIES TEN CENTS. $4.00 PER YEAR IN ADVANCE.

Entered according to Act of Congress, in the Year 1867, by Harper & Brothers, in the Clerk's Office of the District Court for the Southern District of New York.

"THE FIRST VOTE."—Drawn by A. R. Waud.—[See next Page.]

The First Vote, A.R. Waud's wood engraving for *Harper's Weekly* in 1867, showed the future for African Americans.

New Amendments

After the Civil War, the Republican Party controlled Congress and the White House for many years. From 1861 to 1901, all but three presidents were Republicans. They were the "Party of Lincoln," and many people agreed with their policies.

The Republicans were able to achieve many of their platform goals. The Republican-controlled Congress added three new amendments to the Constitution. The Thirteenth Amendment was ratified, or approved, in 1865. It made slavery illegal. The Fourteenth Amendment, ratified in 1868, granted citizenship to those born or naturalized in the United States. The Fifteenth Amendment, ratified in 1870, gave African-American men the right to vote. They could also run for office. Some were elected to very important positions. All of them were Republicans.

Joseph Rainey was from South Carolina. He escaped slavery by boarding a ship bound for Bermuda. After the Civil War, he came back. He helped form the Republican Party in South Carolina. He was the first African-American congressman in the country.

John Mercer Langston served as a township clerk in Ohio in 1855, years before the Civil War. Later, he became the first African-American congressman from Virginia.

Hiram Revels worked as a Methodist minister before the war and as a military recruiter and chaplain during the war. After the war, he worked in politics. He was on the city council in Natchez, Mississippi. Then he served on Mississippi's state legislature. In 1870, he became the first African-American United States Senator. He won the seat that Confederate president Jefferson Davis had held six years before the war.

Joseph Rainey

Despite the new amendments, life for the freed slaves was still not easy. For decades to come, some Southerners, mainly Democrats, tried to prevent African Americans from voting in elections and running for office. African Americans who tried to vote were sometimes beaten or lynched. Republicans were strongly against this type of behavior. They said so, many times, in their official platforms.

Charles Sumner, a Republican senator from Massachusetts, was a big supporter of civil rights for African Americans. He worked most of his career trying to pass laws to help African Americans gain citizenship and equal treatment under the law. Before the Civil War, a pro-slavery congressman, Preston S. Brooks of South Carolina, beat him with a cane until he was unconscious. Years later, on his deathbed, Sumner was still trying to help African Americans. He told a friend, "You must take care of the civil rights bill—my bill, the civil rights bill. Don't let it fail." The next year, the Republican-controlled Congress passed his bill, the 1875 Civil Rights Act.

Woman Suffrage
Republicans believed that every citizen allowed by the Constitution to vote should not be denied the right to vote. It would not matter if this person were rich or poor, black or white. They wanted to make it illegal for anyone to try to prevent a citizen from voting.

Once African-American men could vote, women wondered when they would get suffrage, or the right to vote. They had been asking for it ever since the United States had become a country. Many women dedicated their lives to this cause, and Republicans stood behind them.

Major Issues on Republican Platform, 1870s and 1890s

Gain voting rights for women

Protect the civil rights of African Americans

Provide free education for children

Levy tariffs to protect the interests of U.S. businesses and farmers

Strengthen the military

Protect trade from monopolies

Avoid entangling alliances with other nations and expect other
nations not to meddle in U.S. affairs

Produce money that is backed by gold

Women have been an important part of the Republican Party since the beginning. When the party was formed in Ripon, Wisconsin, three women were there. Women gave speeches and served as delegates at Republican conventions. In 1872, equal rights for women became part of the Republican Party's official platform.

HARPER'S WEEKLY.
JOURNAL OF CIVILIZATION.

Vol. XXVIII.—No. 1420.
Copyright, 1884, by Harper & Brothers.   NEW YORK, SATURDAY, MARCH 8, 1884.   TEN CENTS A COPY.
$4.00 PER YEAR, IN ADVANCE.

REPUBLICAN PARTY.

CIVIL SERVICE

THE SACRED ELEPHANT.
THIS ANIMAL IS SURE TO WIN, IF IT IS ONLY KEPT PURE AND CLEAN, AND HAS NOT TOO HEAVY A LOAD TO CARRY.

The symbol of the Republican Party is the elephant. The nickname is the GOP. Where did these come from and what do they mean?

A cartoonist in New York drew a political cartoon for *Harper's Weekly* about the 1874 election. His name was Thomas Nast (he's in the lower right-hand corner). He showed the Republican Party as an elephant and used the already established donkey for the Democrats. Many other cartoonists liked this idea and started using these symbols in their art, too. The symbols stuck, and both parties still use them today.

The letters *GOP* now mean "Grand Old Party." In 1874, they stood for "Gallant Old Party."

Susan B. Anthony was an important Republican woman. Even though she couldn't vote in elections, she still campaigned for Republican candidates. She spent her life fighting for women's rights. In 1872, she was arrested. She, along with other Republican women, tried to vote in the presidential election. They believed that the Fourteenth Amendment gave them the right to vote. A judge saw it differently. At her trial, he said she was guilty of illegal voting. He didn't even give the jury a chance to say what they thought, which means she didn't get a fair trial.

Since men and women on the western frontier had to work the land if they wanted to survive, men often treated women as their equals. Because of this, women had the right to vote (on city and state issues) in all of the Western states decades before the Nineteenth Amendment was passed.

Years later, in 1920, women were finally given the right to vote. In 1919, a Republican Congress passed the Nineteenth Amendment to the Constitution, and the next year the states ratified it. Anthony did not live to see this day. She died in 1906.

Chapter 3

Dawn of a New Century

In 1903, President Theodore Roosevelt looked out over the south rim in amazement. Orange-red sandstone cliffs glowed in the sunlight. They had been carved over millions of years by the slow-moving waters of the blue-green Colorado River. Even though Roosevelt was an outdoorsman who loved to explore the wilderness, this was the first time he had ever visited the Grand Canyon. He was in awe. After gazing out over the vista, he turned to address the people who had come that day to hear him speak.

"Keep this great wonder of nature as it now is . . . ," he told them. "Keep it for your children, your children's children, and for all who come after you, as one of the great sights which every American if he can travel at all should see."

Roosevelt had always loved nature. As president, he worked hard to make sure the earth and its resources were protected. For this he became known as the Father of Conservation. While in office, he established 5 national parks, 150 national forests, 51 federal bird reserves, 4 national game preserves, 18 national monuments, and 24 reclamation projects.

Theodore Roosevelt established the country's first forest service and saved thousands of acres of land from development.

Roosevelt wasn't the first Republican president to protect the nation's wilderness areas. In 1864, Abraham Lincoln signed an act of Congress that reserved the Yosemite Valley and Mariposa Grove of Giant Sequoias as California state parks. Later, in 1872, President Ulysses S. Grant made Yellowstone the country's first national park. In 1891, Benjamin Harrison signed the Forest Reserve Act, which protected the nation's forests.

Moving Forward

Many consider Theodore Roosevelt to be one of the greatest Republican presidents. In addition to protecting the earth, he also protected people. He considered himself the president for all Americans no matter how rich or poor they were or what kinds of jobs they had. He believed in voting rights for women, fair treatment of workers, and child labor laws.

He went after big companies that weren't doing business fairly. Some companies in the United States had become too big and powerful. Smaller businesses didn't stand a chance against these monopolies, so the big companies had little competition. They could increase prices as they wished. Employers could also treat their workers poorly. Republicans had passed a law in 1890 called the Sherman Antitrust Act that said these companies could not operate this way. Roosevelt forced these companies to obey the law.

He also helped pass the Pure Food and Drug Act. At this time, food factories in the United States were horribly unclean. Meatpacking plants crawled with

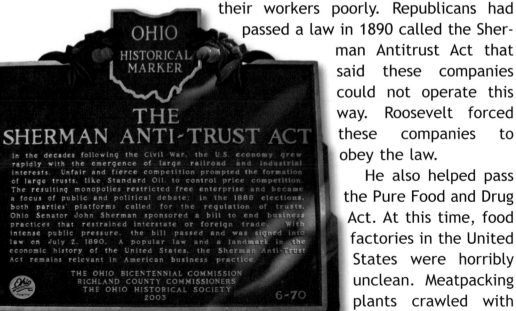

OHIO
HISTORICAL
MARKER

THE
SHERMAN ANTI-TRUST ACT

In the decades following the Civil War, the U.S. economy grew rapidly with the emergence of large railroad and industrial interests. Unfair and fierce competition prompted the formation of large trusts, like Standard Oil, to control price competition. The resulting monopolies restricted free enterprise and became a focus of public and political debate; in the 1888 elections, both parties' platforms called for the regulation of trusts. Ohio Senator John Sherman sponsored a bill to end business practices that restrained interstate or foreign trade. With intense public pressure, the bill passed and was signed into law on July 2, 1890. A popular law and a landmark in the economic history of the United States, the Sherman Anti-Trust Act remains relevant in American business practice.

THE OHIO BICENTENNIAL COMMISSION
RICHLAND COUNTY COMMISSIONERS
THE OHIO HISTORICAL SOCIETY
2003   6-70

rodents. Spoiled and rotten food was often sold to customers. The Pure Food and Drug Act made sure the food that people bought in stores was safe to eat.

Roosevelt also encouraged the construction of the Panama Canal. This would give ships going from the Atlantic to the Pacific a shortcut. Instead of having to go all the way around South America, ships could take a shorter route through the canal in Central America.

Another issue important to Republicans in the early

President Theodore Roosevelt observes the construction of the Panama Canal.

1900s was campaign contributions. A campaign contribution is money that is given as a gift to a candidate to help pay for his or her political campaign. The Republicans wanted to make sure that individuals and big businesses were not giving enormous amounts of money to a candidate. If that person was elected, he or she might feel obligated to help out that business or individual instead of someone who had not given the money. This is still an issue in politics. Laws to change or limit contributions are called campaign finance reform.

Republicans also believed that the United States should stay out of war. If the country was attacked, that would be one thing. But if other countries were fighting with each other, then the United States should stay out of it. Because of this, Republicans did not want to join World War I. And after the war, they did not want the country to be part of the League of Nations.

Of the sixty people who helped form the NAACP (National Association for the Advancement of Colored People) in 1909, two were African-American Republican women: Mary Terrell and Ida Wells-Barnett.

The Calm Before the Storm

The 1920s were a time of prosperity for many people in the United States. Women got the right to vote. Many people had jobs; the unemployment rate was low. The automobile became popular. Homes and businesses had electricity. Aviators like Charles Lindbergh and Amelia Earhart began flying airplanes. People could listen to the radio at home, or they could spend a quarter to see a silent movie in the theater.

Republicans adapted their platform to these new issues. They felt that roadways should be built so that people could easily drive their cars from place to place. They wanted every home in America to have a radio. They thought airplanes should be used to move mail, goods, and people.

Although the 1920s were prosperous, many Americans made poor choices with their money. They bought on credit, promising to pay later. This seemed okay at the time because they had jobs. But what would happen if they lost their jobs or could no longer work? Where would they get the money to pay their debts?

In 1928, the Republicans included this issue in their platform. They said that people needed to start spending wisely and saving wisely. But for many people, this advice came too late. On October 29, 1929, the stock market crashed. Businesses failed. Banks closed. Factories went bankrupt. Millions of people lost their jobs and became homeless. The Great Depression had started.

There were three Republican presidents during the 1920s: Warren G. Harding, Calvin Coolidge, and Herbert C. Hoover. Because Hoover was president when the stock market crashed, many people blamed him and the Republicans for the Great Depression. *Hoover*

Major Issues on Republican Platform, 1930s and 1940s

Limit the number of terms a president can serve
Balance the budget
Reduce taxes
Care for veterans and their families
Establish unemployment insurance
Care for the elderly
Support the efforts of the United Nations
Prevent government competition with private businesses
Promote civil rights for African Americans (in society and military)
End monopolies; support small businesses
Build a strong military

became a negative term. When people had to wrap themselves in newspapers to keep warm, they called these "Hoover blankets." When people had to live in shacks built out of scraps, their new makeshift towns were called "Hoovervilles."

The Republican platforms during the 1930s were filled with many ideas of how to get the country through this crisis. But many people had already lost faith in the Republicans. In the election of 1932, Democrat Franklin Delano Roosevelt won the presidency. Democrats won the majority in Congress, too. The Republicans would not play a significant role in American politics again until the 1950s.

Hooverville in Sacramento, California

Rolling Into the Fifties

On July 7, 1919, a train pulled out of Washington, D.C., and began its long journey westward toward California. This wasn't a typical train that snaked along tracks made of iron rails. Instead, it was a train made up of 81 military vehicles: trucks, cars, motorcycles, ambulances, and tractors. The train was on a mission for the government. The army personnel were to find out just how good—or bad—America's roads, bridges, and tunnels really were.

It took this train sixty-two days to travel from coast to coast. The military found roads in all kinds of conditions. Some were good paved roads. Others were dirt roads. Farther west, the roads faded into bumpy old wagon trails through prairies, deserts, and mountains. The train had more than 230 breakdowns and accidents along the way: trucks ran off the road, sank in sand, and slipped off muddy trails. At the end of the journey, the army reported its findings. America's roads definitely needed to be improved!

One of the army officers on this truck train never forgot the experience. His name was Dwight D. Eisenhower. Thirty-four years later he was elected president

"There must be no second-class citizens in this country."
—Dwight D. Eisenhower

of the United States. Fixing America's roads became one of his top priorities. On June 29, 1956, President Eisenhower signed the Federal-Aid Highway Act. This law gave $25 billion so that 41,000 miles of highways could be built across America. The extensive interstate system built under this act is still used today.

"I Like Ike"

Eisenhower is considered one of the top four Republican presidents, along with Lincoln, Theodore Roosevelt, and Ronald Reagan. Elected in 1952, he brought to the White House a new kind of Republican Party called Modern Republicanism.

During the Great Depression, Democratic president Franklin Delano Roosevelt set up economic and social programs called the New Deal. Many Republicans disliked anything to do with the New Deal. Eisenhower felt differently. While he felt that some New Deal programs should go, he also felt that some should stay, such as minimum wage, unemployment insurance, and social security. He agreed with traditional Republican ideas, though. For example, he believed that government should stay out of business and, except for outlawing monopolies, let the free market grow on its own.

Like many Republicans before him, Eisenhower was a champion for human rights. He signed the Civil Rights Acts of 1957 and 1960.

President Dwight D. Eisenhower signing the Civil Rights Act of 1957. He is famous for saying, "I believe as long as we allow conditions to exist that make for second-class citizens, we are making of ourselves less than first-class citizens."

Major Issues on Republican Platform, 1950s and 1960s

Prevent communism from spreading

Support the United Nations

Support the State of Israel as a Jewish homeland

Lower the national debt; lower taxes

Care for veterans and their families

Care for the elderly

Vote against federal health insurance

Ensure equal education for all children

Prevent government competition with private businesses

Promote civil rights for all Americans

Support small businesses and workers

Promote a strong military

Now, anyone who tried to prevent African Americans from voting could be punished. In 1957, Eisenhower also had to make a decision on the issue of segregation. In *Brown v. Board of Education*, the Supreme Court had ruled that segregating—keeping white and black students in separate schools—was unconstitutional. Many southerners did not want to change, though, and riots erupted in Little Rock when Central High School was integrated. Eisenhower had no choice but to send federal troops on September 24, 1957, to uphold the Constitution.

Fear of Communism

After World War II ended, the Cold War began. This wasn't a war of death and destruction. Instead, it was a war of words that everyone feared could easily turn deadly. Democracy and

Republican Hiram Fong was the country's first Asian-American U.S. Senator. He represented Hawaii when it became a state in 1959.

communism were facing off, with the United States on one side and the Soviet Union on the other. Many people in the United States feared that communism would spread around the world. It was already in the Soviet Union, Eastern Europe, China, North Korea, and Cuba—which was very close to home. Nuclear weapons caused a great amount of fear during the Cold War, too. Both the United States and the Soviet Union had atomic bombs. If words turned to action, the result could be devastating.

The fear of communism and nuclear war changed Republican foreign policy. The party now believed that the United States had to stop the Soviets from spreading communism around the world. If they had to use force to do that, they should. This idea was shared by the Democrats, too. During this time, the Cold War turned into real war twice, once in Korea and once in Vietnam. U.S. soldiers fought to stop the communist takeovers in those countries. In Korea it worked, since South Korea remained a democracy. In Vietnam it did not. The communists took over the entire country when the American forces pulled out.

Joseph McCarthy was a Republican senator from Wisconsin. He had a deep fear and hatred for communism. In fact, he believed that there were commu- nists all over the United States who were working as spies to take over the government. He be- lieved it was his job to hunt these people down and arrest them.

U.S. Senator Joseph McCarthy testifies before a Senate subcommittee as he tries to link fellow senator William Benton to communism.

During the 1950s, he falsely accused a lot of people, including writers, scientists, politicians, and Hollywood movie stars. His actions have often been described as a witch hunt. Before he was stopped, hundreds of people lost their jobs. He caused a lot of serious problems for the country and became an embarrassment to the Republican Party.

Watergate

Another embarrassment for the Republican Party was the Watergate scandal. It involved President Richard Nixon. He was afraid that people would try to make him look foolish or claim he said things that he didn't say. When he was elected president, he installed tape recorders in the Oval Office. That way, he would have proof of everything he said. This might have seemed like a good idea to him at the time, but it actually brought about his ruin.

During a broadcast of his address to the nation, Nixon reads from the edited transcripts of the Nixon White House Tape conversations.

Republican Margaret Chase Smith of Maine was the first woman to be elected to both houses of Congress. In 1964, she became the first woman to be seriously considered for the presidential nomination by a major political party.

Major Issues on Republican Platform, 1970s

End the war in Vietnam

Broker peace in the Middle East

Limit nuclear weapons

Begin trading with China

Institute an all-volunteer military; eliminate the draft

Ensure quality healthcare at a reasonable cost

Improve education

Reform the welfare program

Leave the children of America a legacy of clean air, clean water, vast open spaces, and easily accessible parks

Keep illegal drugs out of the country

In 1972, he was running for reelection. Some of his campaign people broke into the Democratic National Headquarters at the Watergate Hotel in Washington. They claimed they were just trying to find out the Democrats' ideas for the campaign—but the break-in was still illegal. President Nixon insisted he didn't know anything about it. Investigators asked for the tapes from the Oval Office. When they got them, a section of the recording was missing. It looked as if President Nixon was trying to cover up something. He was in big trouble, and he knew it. Instead of going to trial, he resigned on August 4, 1974. One month later, the man who took his place in office, Gerald Ford, pardoned him.

Nixon had done a lot of good things while in office. He had formed the Environmental Protection Agency (EPA). He had helped end the war in Vietnam. He opened the door for trade with China by becoming the first U.S. president to visit there. Despite the positive things he accomplished, though, Nixon is mainly remembered for the Watergate scandal.

Key Republicans

Barry Goldwater served as senator from Arizona for thirty years. He was highly against FDR's New Deal because he believed it made the federal government too powerful. For that he became known as Mr. Conservative. He was the Republican presidential candidate for the 1964 election. Ronald Reagan gave speeches across the country to help with his campaign.

Henry Kissinger (right) was a close adviser to President Ford. In fact, Kissinger was one of the first people that Ford called when he became president in 1974.

Henry Kissinger served as national security adviser and secretary of state for both Richard Nixon and Gerald Ford. He was an expert on foreign policy. He helped negotiate peace at the end of the Vietnam War, for which he received the 1973 Nobel Peace Prize. He helped open up discussions and trade between the United States and China. He also initiated the policy of détente with the Soviet Union. This easing of tension between the two countries allowed them to begin to work out agreements peacefully. It opened the door for the negotiations of the 1980s.

"Tear Down This Wall"

On June 12, 1987, Ronald Reagan—in his second term in office—stood in front of Brandenburg Gate by the infamous Berlin Wall. After World War II, the German capital had been divided into communist East Berlin and democratic West Berlin. In the 1960s, the Soviet Union, which governed East Berlin, erected a cement wall to permanently separate the two sides of the city. East Berliners were denied many freedoms and were forced to live under communist rule.

On this day, Reagan talked about freedom, democracy, and the failures of communism. Then he spoke directly to Mikhail Gorbachev, the leader of the Soviet Union.

"General Secretary Gorbachev," he said. "If you seek peace, if you seek prosperity for the Soviet Union and Eastern Europe, if you seek liberalization: Come here to this gate! Mr. Gorbachev, open this gate! Mr. Gorbachev, tear down this wall!"

Reagan was known as the Great Communicator. When he talked, people listened, and many respected what he had to say. His ability to communicate helped him as he discussed peace with the Soviet Union. It also helped him win both his elections. For his first

In 1987, President Ronald Reagan gave an impassioned speech against communism in front of the Brandenburg Gate.

term in office, he won by a landslide. He received 489 electoral votes. His opponent, President Jimmy Carter, received only 49. For his second term, he won with an even greater margin: 525 electoral votes to his opponent's 13. The Democrats who voted for him became known as Reagan Democrats.

Reagan based his politics on two basic ideals. One: free the nation from big government. Two: free the world from communism. He also increased employment, lowered taxes, strengthened defense forces, and lowered government spending. He encouraged research in science and technology, especially with the space program. He wanted people to rely less on government and more on their own abilities. He believed in peace through strength. He met with Soviet leaders many times, and showed the United States as a powerful nation that championed freedom for all people.

Eventually, the people in the Soviet Union broke free of communist rule. On November 9, 1989, two years after Reagan left office, communism in East Berlin ended. People from around the world watched on television as Berliners from both sides climbed on the wall and tore it down piece by piece.

George H. W. Bush served as Reagan's vice president for eight years. Then, in 1989, he was elected president. He was president when the Berlin Wall came down. In 1990, Iraqi dictator Saddam

Mikhail Gorbachev (left) and President Ronald Reagan signing the Intermediate-Range Nuclear Forces Treaty of 1987. This treaty reduced the threat of nuclear war.

Major Issues on Republican Platform, 1980s and 1990s

Eliminate barriers for Americans with disabilities

Promote rights for unborn children

Promote strong families as the basis of democracy

Provide quality education for all children

Vote against publicly funded healthcare

Improve neighborhoods, with neighbors helping neighbors

Reduce the role of the federal government

Lower taxes

Fund research in science and technology

Promote soil and water conservation

Wage war on drugs: Just Say No! campaign

Hussein invaded Kuwait. In response, Bush sent troops to the Persian Gulf. He called the military action Operation Desert Storm.

Entering the Twenty-first Century

George H.W. Bush

In the year 2000, Republican governor of Texas George W. Bush became president of the United States. This election was not typical, though. On election night, the media announced that Democrat Al Gore had won. Minutes later, they said that Bush had won. Florida precincts began recounting their ballots, but the Supreme Court stopped them. Gore had won the popular vote across the country, but Bush had won more votes in the Electoral College.

George W. Bush, who is the son of George H. W. Bush, served two terms in the White House. During his presidency, he championed the No Child Left Behind Act, which attempted to raise standards in America's public schools. He also encouraged free trade agreements, increased benefits for Medicare patients, and increased government support for veterans.

The most important moment of George W. Bush's presidency, though, occurred on September 11, 2001. On that fateful day, a group of terrorists hijacked four commercial airliners. They used these planes as bombs and flew them into buildings. Two went into the World Trade Center towers in New York City. Another flew into the Pentagon in Washington, D.C. It is believed that the fourth plane was targeting the White House. Its passengers, who already knew what happened in New York, foiled the terrorists' plans and

President George W. Bush gives a speech in New York City on September 14, 2001, where the Twin Towers were destroyed by terrorist attacks just three days prior.

retook the plane. They crashed it into empty farmland in Pennsylvania.

September 11, also known as 9/11, changed everything for the Bush administration. As Condoleezza Rice, the national security adviser, said, "For those of us in office on that day, it is as if time was suspended. For us and for the victims' families, every day since then has been September 12." Bush and his advisers felt their job was to keep Americans safe. Their plans for protection included passing the PATRIOT Act and tightening security at airports and border crossings.

Important Republicans from the 1980s and Beyond

For the first time in forty years, the Republicans had enough seats in the House of Representatives to name one of their own as Speaker of the House. In fact, in 1994, they won the majority not only in the House, but also in the Senate. Newt Gingrich served as Speaker from 1995 to 1999. He worked to oppose the policies of the democratic Clinton administration.

Colin Powell was a four-star general who served as Chairman of the Joint Chiefs of Staff from 1989 to 1993. This is the highest military position in the Department of Defense. He led the armed forces in Operation Desert Storm. He also led them in the invasion of Panama to remove General Manuel Noriega from power. Later, from 2001 to 2005, Powell served as secretary of state. He was the first African American to hold this position.

General Colin Powell

Condoleezza Rice was the national security adviser for George W. Bush during 9/11. During his

As George W. Bush's national security adviser, Condoleezza Rice counseled the president on matters of national security. This position was extremely important following the days after 9/11.

second term, from 2005 to 2009, she served as secretary of state. She was the first female African American to serve in this position.

Rudy Giuliani was mayor of New York City from 1994 to 2001. During his administration, he greatly improved the city, making it a safer, cleaner place to live and visit. He was mayor during 9/11. His leadership during the tragedy was so impressive that he received many awards, including honorary knighthood from England's Queen Elizabeth II (which he accepted on behalf of the citizens of New York).

A Remarkable Legacy
Over the years, the Republican Party has adapted with a changing America. Republicans fought to free the slaves. They helped Afri-

As Republicans tried to retake the White House in 2012, presidential hopefuls Mitt Romney (left) and Newt Gingrich (right) compete for the Republican Party nomination.

can Americans, Native Americans, and women obtain the right to vote. They worked to protect the environment, care for veterans, improve education, and build railroads and highways. They helped people around the world gain freedom from harsh and unfair governments.

Since the party was founded in 1854 until the time of this writing, thirty presidents have been elected to the White House. Eighteen of them were Republicans. Men and women of all races have served as Republican mayors, senators, representatives, governors, and cabinet members. Throughout the country, Republicans have also worked hard in their homes, jobs, and communities to make the United States a better place for all people.

The Republican Party has a remarkable legacy. With the strength of its leadership, supporters, and values, the party can continue to make a difference in the country and the world for many more generations.

1854 In March, the Republican Party is formed in a Ripon, Wisconsin, schoolhouse. The Kansas-Nebraska Act is passed. Abraham Lincoln first debates Stephen A. Douglas.

1856 John C. Fremont is nominated as the first Republican candidate for U.S. president.

1860 Abraham Lincoln is elected first Republican president of the United States.

1862 Republican Congress passes the Homestead Act, Pacific Railroad Acts, and Morrill Act.

1863 Construction on Transcontinental Railroad begins.

1864 Lincoln signs an act reserving Yosemite and Mariposa Grove as California state parks.

1865 The Civil War ends on April 9. On April 14, Lincoln is shot; he dies the next day. In December, the Thirteenth Amendment is passed; it outlaws slavery.

1868 The Fourteenth Amendment is passed, granting citizenship to those born or naturalized in the United States.

1869 The Transcontinental Railroad is completed.

1870 The Fifteenth Amendment is passed, granting all male citizens the right to vote; the next day, Thomas Mundy Peterson becomes the first African American to vote.

1872 Republican party includes women's right to vote on its official platform; Susan B. Anthony is arrested for voting illegally; Ulysses S. Grant makes Yellowstone the country's first national park.

1874 The elephant becomes the Republican Party symbol and GOP its nickname.

1875 The Civil Rights Act is passed.

1890 The Sherman Antitrust Act is passed, outlawing monopolies.

1892 Republicans include the protection of civil rights on their official platform.

1903 Theodore Roosevelt visits the Grand Canyon for the first time.

1920 The Nineteenth Amendment, giving women the right to vote, is added to the Constitution.

1924 The Indian Citizenship Act gives Native Americans the right to vote.

1929 On October 29, the stock market crashes, and the Great Depression begins.

1932 Republicans lose the presidency and power in Congress; they will not play a significant role in either for twenty years.

1952 Republican Dwight D. Eisenhower is elected president.

1956 Eisenhower signs the Federal-Aid Highway Act to improve interstate travel.

1957 The Civil Rights Act of 1957 establishes a civil rights division in the Justice Department.

1959 Hiram Fong becomes the first Asian-American U.S. Senator.

1960 The Civil Rights Act of 1960 strengthens the provisions of earlier civil rights laws.

1964 Margaret Chase Smith is seriously considered for Republican presidential candidate.

1972 President Richard Nixon goes to China.

1974 Nixon resigns because of the Watergate scandal. Gerald Ford becomes president.

1987 Ronald Reagan speaks at Brandenburg Gate at the Berlin Wall.

1994 Republicans win the majority in the House and Senate. Newt Gingrich becomes Speaker of the House.

2000 George W. Bush wins the presidency over Al Gore after an extremely close election.

2001 On September 11, terrorists hijack airplanes and fly them into buildings in New York and Washington, D.C. Hijackers on a fourth plane are thwarted in Shanksville, Pennsylvania. Bush declares a War on Terror. Operation Enduring Freedom begins with airstrikes against Afghanistan on October 7.

2003 U.S. troops enter Iraq in March as part of Operation Iraqi Freedom.

2004 Bush's popularity begins to decline as people criticize how he handles domestic and foreign policy issues, including his response to Hurricane Katrina and the War on Terror.

2011 While Democratic president Barack Obama is in his third year in office, Americans vote more Republicans to Congress.

2012 Campaigning begins for the 2012 national election.

Republican Presidents

Name	Number in the Order of the Presidents	Dates in Office
Abraham Lincoln	16	1861–1865
Ulysses S. Grant	18	1869–1877
Rutherford B. Hayes	19	1877–1881
James Garfield	20	1881
Chester A. Arthur	21	1881–1885
Benjamin Harrison	23	1889–1893
William McKinley	25	1897–1901
Theodore Roosevelt	26	1901–1909
William Howard Taft	27	1909–1913
Warren G. Harding	29	1921–1923
Calvin Coolidge	30	1923–1929
Herbert C. Hoover	31	1929–1933
Dwight D. Eisenhower	34	1953–1961
Richard M. Nixon	37	1969–1974
Gerald R. Ford	38	1974–1977
Ronald Reagan	40	1981–1989
George H. W. Bush	41	1989–1993
George W. Bush	43	2001–2009

Books

Anderson, Dale. *The Republican Party: The Story of the Grand Old Party.* Mankato, MN: Compass Point Books, 2007.

Herbert, Janis. *Abraham Lincoln for Kids: His Life and Times with 21 Activities.* Chicago: Chicago Review Press, 2007.

Hollihan, Kerrie Logan. *Theodore Roosevelt for Kids: His Life and Times with 21 Activities.* Chicago: Chicago Review Press, 2010.

Perritano, John. *Graphic America: Radical Republicans.* New York: Crabtree Publishing Company, 2008.

Wagner, Heather Lehr. *The History of the Republican Party.* New York: Chelsea House Publishers, 2007.

Works Consulted

American Presidency Project. http://www.presidency.ucsb.edu/

American President: Dwight D. Eisenhower. http://millercenter.org/president/eisenhower/essays/biography/4

American Red Cross Museum: "Clara Barton: Founder of the American Red Cross." http://www.redcross.org/museum/history/claraBarton.asp

Barnes, Bart. "Barry Goldwater, GOP Hero, Dies." *Washington Post,* May 30, 1998. http://www.washingtonpost.com/wp-srv/politics/daily/may98/goldwater30.htm

Black Americans in Congress: "John Mercer Langston, Representative, 1890–1891, Republican from Virginia." http://baic.house.gov/member-profiles/profile.html?intID=18

DiPeso, Jim. "The Ten Biggest Republican Environmental Accomplishments." *The Daily Green,* n.d. http://www.thedailygreen.com/environmental-news/latest/republican-environmental-47061502

Documenting the American South: "Frederick Douglass, 1818–1895." http://docsouth.unc.edu/neh/douglass/bio.html

Eisenhower Library: "The 1919 Transcontinental Motor Convoy." http://www.eisenhower.archives.gov/research/audiovisual/images/1919_convoy.html

Flower, Frank A. *History of the Republican Party: Embracing Its Origin, Growth, and Mission.* Grand Rapids, MI: Union Book Company, 1884.

Foner, Eric. *Free Soil, Free Labor, Free Men: The Ideology of the Republican Party Before the Civil War.* New York: Oxford University Press, 1970.

GOP Heroes. http://www.gop.com/index.php/issues/heroes/

Gould, Lewis L. *Grand Old Party: A History of the Republicans.* New York: Random House, 2003.

Grant, Ulysses S. "Reasons for Being a Republican." http://www.bartleby.com/268/10/13.html

"Guiliani Receives Honorary Knighthood." *Daily Mail Online,* February 13, 2002. http://www.dailymail.co.uk/news/article-100049/Guiliani-receives-honorary-knighthood.html

Henry A. Kissinger. http://www.henryakissinger.com/

Lenti, Sarah. "Every Day Since Then Has Been September 12." *NMPolitics,* September 10, 2011. http://www.nmpolitics.net/index/2011/09/every-day-since-then-has-been-sept-12/

The Lincoln Institute: Mr. Lincoln and Freedom, "Pre-Civil War." http://www.mrlincolnandfreedom.org/inside.asp?ID=10&subjectID=2

The Lincoln Log: "A Daily Chronology of the Life of Abraham Lincoln." http://www.thelincolnlog.org/view/1854/10

Linder, Doug. "The Trial of Susan B. Anthony for Illegal Voting." 2001. http://law2.umkc.edu/faculty/projects/ftrials/anthony/sbaaccount.html

Livingstone, William. *Livingstone's History of the Republican Party.* Detroit, MI: Wm. Livingstone, 1900.

Long, John D. *The Republican Party: Its History, Principles, and Policies.* New York: M.W. Hazen Company, 1888.

McGinnis, William C. *The History of Perth Amboy, New Jersey.* Perth Amboy, NJ: American Publishing Company, 1958–1962. http://slic.njstatelib.org/slic_files/digidocs/Jerseyana/J923p458.pdf

National Federation of Republican Women: "Women and the GOP—Suffrage." http://www.nfrw.org/republicans/women/suffrage.htm

National Park Service: "Theodore Roosevelt—Presidential Accomplishments." http://www.nps.gov/history/logcabin/html/tr3.html

PBS: Africans in America: "Frederick Douglass, 1818–1895." http://www.pbs.org/wgbh/aia/part4/4p1539.html

Pfeiffer, David A. "Ike's Interstates at 50: Anniversary of the Highway System Recalls Eisenhower's Role as Catalyst." *Prologue Magazine,* Summer 2006. http://www.archives.gov/publications/prologue/2006/summer/interstates.html

Picture Show Man: "How Much Did It Cost to See a Movie During the 1920s?" http://www.pictureshowman.com/questionsandanswers4.cfm#Q19

Political Speeches and Debates of Abraham Lincoln and Stephen A. Douglas, 1854–1861: "The Missouri Compromise." http://www.archive.org/stream/politicalspeeche2774linc#page/n15/mode/2up

Race, Voting Rights, and Segregation: "Rise and Fall of the Black Voter, 1868–1922." http://www.umich.edu/~lawrace/votetour2.htm

Reagan, Ronald. "Acceptance Speech at the 1980 Republican Convention." July 17, 1980. http://www.nationalcenter.org/ReaganConvention1980.html

———. "A Time for Choosing." Campaign speech for Barry Goldwater, 1964. http://video.google.com/videoplay?docid=-1777069922535499977

Reagan at Brandenburg Gate—"Tear Down This Wall." http://www.youtube.com/watch?v=YtYdjbpBk6A

"Suffrage Wins in Senate; Now Goes to States." *The New York Times,* June 5, 1919. http://www.fordham.edu/halsall/mod/1920womensvote.html

Susan B. Anthony House. http://susanbanthonyhouse.org/index.php

Theodore Roosevelt Association. http://www.theodoreroosevelt.org/life/conservation.htm

University of Washington. *The Great Depression in Washington State*: "Hoovervilles and Homelessness." http://depts.washington.edu/depress/hooverville.shtml

U.S. Department of Transportation, Federal Highway Administration: "President Dwight D. Eisenhower Audio Gallery." http://www.fhwa.dot.gov/interstate/audiogallery.htm

USHistory.org: "Republican Philadelphia—Origins of the Republican Party." http://www.ushistory.org/gop/origins.htm

White, Horace. *Abraham Lincoln in 1854.* http://www.archive.org/stream/abrahamlincolnin00whit/abrahamlincolnin00whit_djvu.txt

The White House: The Presidents. http://www.whitehouse.gov/about/presidents/

Wisconsin Historical Society: "Wisconsin and the Republican Party." http://www.wisconsinhistory.org/turningpoints/tp-022/?action=more_essay

On the Internet

ACLU: Voting Rights Act Timeline—http://www.aclu.org/voting-rights/voting-rights-act-timeline

Congress For Kids, Political Parties—http://www.congressforkids.net/Elections_politicalparties.htm

National Archives—http://www.archives.gov/

PBS: Transcontinental Railroad—http://www.pbs.org/wgbh/americanexperience/films/tcrr/

Republican National Committee—http://www.gop.com

Republican Party Historical Society—http://republicanpartyhistoricalsociety.org/

Voice of America: "Movies Become Big Business in the 1920s." December 7, 2010. http://www.voanews.com/learningenglish/theclassroom/articles/american_history/Movies-Become-Big-Business-in-the-1920s-111456524.html

bipartisan (by-PAR-tih-zin)—Involving two parties working together or compromising on an issue.

campaign finance reform (kam-PAYN FY-nants ree-FORM)—Efforts to prevent political candidates from taking too much money as contributions from one particular person or organization, since that could lead to bribery and corruption.

child labor law—A series of laws passed in the early 1900s that prohibited children under a certain age from working. Today, this age is 16 years old. These laws were also designed to protect children who were old enough to work from unsafe working conditions, long hours, and unfair wages.

convention (kun-VEN-shun)—An assembly of people for a specific purpose.

desegregation (dee-seh-greh-GAY-shun)—The stopping of segregation, or purposeful separation, of groups of people.

détente (day-TAHNT)—The relaxing of strained tensions between nations.

lynch (LINCH)—To kill a person who is not convicted of a crime, usually done by a mob and by hanging.

monopoly (mah-NAH-puh-lee)—The exclusive ownership, possession, or control of a particular supply or service.

pardon (PAR-dun)—The excusing of an offense without giving a penalty.

party (PAR-tee)—An organization formed with the goal of gaining political power. Members of the party generally share the same beliefs and views on specific issues.

platform (PLAT-form)—A political party's official stance on issues.

precinct (PREE-sinkt)—One of the divisions in a county, town, or city made for election purposes.

Soviet Union (SOH-vee-ut YOON-yun)—The shorter name for the Union of Soviet Socialist Republics (USSR), a group of communist countries that was unified from 1922 to 1991. It included Russia and surrounding countries that today make up Armenia, Azerbaijan, Belarus, Estonia, Georgia, Kazakhstan, Kyrgyzstan, Latvia, Lithuania, Moldova, Tajikistan, Turkmenistan, Ukraine, and Uzbekistan.

suffrage (SUH-fridj)—The right to vote.

About the Author

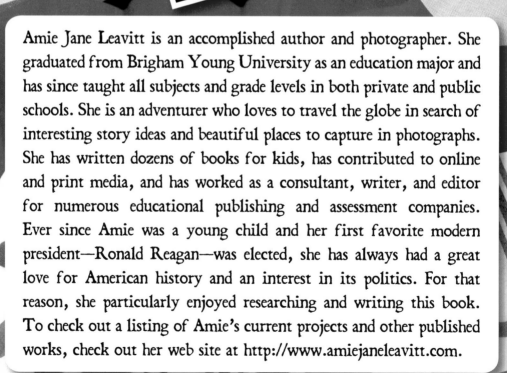

Amie Jane Leavitt is an accomplished author and photographer. She graduated from Brigham Young University as an education major and has since taught all subjects and grade levels in both private and public schools. She is an adventurer who loves to travel the globe in search of interesting story ideas and beautiful places to capture in photographs. She has written dozens of books for kids, has contributed to online and print media, and has worked as a consultant, writer, and editor for numerous educational publishing and assessment companies. Ever since Amie was a young child and her first favorite modern president—Ronald Reagan—was elected, she has always had a great love for American history and an interest in its politics. For that reason, she particularly enjoyed researching and writing this book. To check out a listing of Amie's current projects and other published works, check out her web site at http://www.amiejaneleavitt.com.